Antinopolis

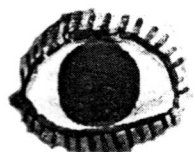

ELIZABETH PARKER
Antinopolis

EYEWEAR  AVIATOR
2016 SERIES

First published in 2016
by Eyewear Publishing Ltd
Suite 333, 19-21 Crawford Street
Marylebone, London W1H 1PJ
United Kingdom

Typeset with graphic design by Edwin Smet
Printed in England by Lightning Source
All rights reserved © 2016 Elizabeth Parker

The right of Elizabeth Parker to be identified as author of this work has been asserted in accordance with section 77 of the Copyright, Designs and Patents Act 1988

ISBN 978-1-908998-79-8

Eyewear wishes to thank Jonathan Wonham for his very generous patronage of our press.

WWW.EYEWEARPUBLISHING.COM

Many thanks to
The Spoke – Claire Williamson, Robert Walton and Paul Deaton
for all their support and encouragement.

Antinopolis

A city founded by the Roman emperor
Hadrian to commemorate his deified young
beloved Antinous, who drowned in the Nile.

The site of excavations by French explorer
Albert Gayet, who discovered 'Mummy Portraits'
at the site – highly realistic head-and-shoulder
portraits attached to mummies of the Coptic period,
bound into the burial cloth so as to cover the face
of the deceased and painted in the classical
style of ancient Greece and Rome.

Table of contents

- 9   Antinopolis
- 11   Wife
- 12   His Father's Eye
- 14   The Falling Man 9/11
- 15   Donors
- 16   My Mother and The Mysteries
- 17   Reading Owen
- 18   Lower Intermediate, August
- 19   Home
- 20   That Night
- 21   West Pier, Brighton
- 22   At Cannop Ponds
- 24   This Pool
- 25   Free Morning
- 26   Bertha
- 27   Let The Breeze In
- 28   Grandad
- 29   Mistress
- 30   His Groom
- 31   The Word

- 33   Acknowledgements

Antinopolis

They have locked up the river where you fell
bike-tyre slotting into tramline, tipping you

into water that wants us all
now striped with chrome bars.

There is a photo in a pollypocket
cable-tied to a tube bolt.

Your looks were classical
remind me of the mummified boy
in Antinopolis
his portrait on a cedar panel
bright lips, thick brush strokes of black hair.

When Albert Gayet opened the dark
their faces gleamed in the tombs
ancient paint still glossy
in egg-yolk eyes, milk cheeks

hair of soot and plant gum
lips a pinch of cinnabar
stirred through beeswax
kept hot and dry
for two thousand years.

After two years
your shrine is fading

carnations threaded through the bars
hemmed brown with rot

rain drawing pale lines
through your inkjet colours.

I want to laminate your picture
so your face shines

unpick metal stitches
slimy weave of dead carnations.

Wife

She has left her peelings on the bed
silk dress, pineapple yellow
pith of white lace.

Creases are closed lips.
I kneel, part folds
for trace scent. Prada Amber

blended, perhaps, with another man's breath
standing so close his shadow cooled her arm
darkened the silk.

'More like spray paint than fabric'
I had whispered while I zipped
drew a chilly line up her spine.

Now I listen to the hiss of the shower
and wait

her silk waist clenched
in the tube of my fist.

His Father's Eye

'Mum said there's a man at the memorial
with your daddy's eye.'

Adam told me the story during our lunch hour
that smelt of *Golden Virginia* and sawdust.

He lowered his voice when he explained
he'd checked the one close-up she'd framed
found their eyes were the same.
'Sewage eyes – all the crappest colours.'

While he chewed cold pasta I found bits of gold
a caramel corona in his iris.

He told me his mum and two friends
had giggled in the hospital room
watching the final salute rise up beneath the sheets
as the ventilator shut down.
'She just couldn't cry anymore at that point.'

I stared at his fingers' stained tips
as he glided the last pasta twist
gathered a red slick of sauce
and we both caught the airtight click of his Tupperware.

Salute lowered, sheet stilled.
'Two taps on her shoulder
and his voice –
Don't forget I'm a donor.'

There is a raisin scent of toasted tobacco,
rustle as Adam pinches brown strands
sprinkles them on paper, rolls, licks.

At first bell
his fingers on my shoulderbone,
low voice even quieter:

'Like this.'

The Falling Man 9/11

A 'life assembly'
'Wyoming 64 million years'
trapped shoal dead in seconds

water, minerals sliding into spaces
left as their bones dissolved
until someone tapped a chisel butt
sank an iron tooth into limestone.

Our breath on glass
shrank as it cooled.

I thought of him again
preserved in shivering pixels

bending a knee
white shirt lifting
and how any one of us
could have our names typed for years

beneath one date.

Donors

We push our arms under hoods
humming with extractor fans
that suck loose cells from our hands

snap on new skins
spritz them with ethanol
tape latex gloves to our cuffs
blocking chinks of flesh

draw disinfected breaths
alcohol, bleach, warm yeast
from incubators

cut and lift the cornea
a lid off a white bowl
swilling its eye

wait as it shudders and stills
slice the sclera
splay it like a lily
pick and lift the iris
a large drip stretching from tweezers

our own pupils opening
to pincer a gleam of lens.

We pipette fluids to reach the retina
pry up a red filigree
frail as veins from a leaf

deliver their gifts
wrapped in saline.

My Mother and The Mysteries

My mother and her best friend
went to the woods
'to try out the mysteries.'

They returned with damp hair
pine needles spearing the coils
of their spiral perms.

I watched their grazes
seed the white carpet
their blood sprouting in plush.

They drew trains of bristling air.
I unpicked the weave
found sweat, wine, sap.

Their laughter spooked the cat
and when my mother said goodnight
the word had a new smell.

Reading Owen
After Wilfred Owen's 'Futility'

Each year teachers move him into the sun
scanned from old Fabers

onto high-grade paper
warm from the copier, new as milk.

Children touch words
pencil notes like new shoots.

Beneath fingertips glowing blood
the soldier's skin melts

ice relaxes
rolls into melting hair

heels of new hands
warm his mouth, thaw his lips.

They unpeel an eye
see clouds slip on a green iris

wait for him to resurface.

Lower Intermediate, August

Twelve Russian teenagers
a thread of Levis, diamante and loud whispers
drawn through Coleman's Garden one evening
after management banned lessons outdoors.

I'd stuck words to statues and trees
bark sinking into blue tack
yew, minkha, ginko, maple
plucked down by expensive fingernails
French manicures, stick-on rhinestones.

Twelve Russian teenagers pressed lips
tapped tongue to hard palates
lisped through whitened teeth
for plum, pear and plinth

mispronounced once, stuffed into pockets
or shed from glitzy fingers
to leech moisture from fledged leaves
mulch until trees drank their own names.

Home

He flicks a plastic catch
picks over his tools.

She paints her nails the best blue
Barry M turquoise.

He sits a spirit level on a floating shelf
checks it's flush.

She breathes stillness into lacquer
waits, touches to test
sinks a fingerprint into paint
licks it smooth, waits again.

He swears at a screwdriver
slipping its slot in the screwhead.

She drips paint into a nick
watches it spread, settle, fix.

He drops the screws
lets the shelf slump.

When the polish chips she will peel her fingertips
leave soft shells in the shower.

That Night

when you leant over me to turn the radio dial,
re-tune in our midnight bedroom, finding sitar-
plucked strings flicking molecules of air
in a studio somewhere –

turning again, sliding through
stations, to settle on a string adagio –
hearing low voices in the kitchen
through gaps between the boards.

Our clothes, piled on chair backs,
were like giant crows with wooden bones,
and I licked the perfume from your throat,
savouring your dab of Chanel,

my bitter tongue lifting as you hummed along,
tracking vibrations to your lips.

West Pier, Brighton

Promenade gone, its lovers are cut off
left to collect up broken lines
rebuild it with their eyes
put back columns already auctioned.

They have started a petition to save it
this black clutter spindly as a shrimp
we could snap between fingers.

It is more like a quick sketch
than threaded columns of cast iron.
We could smudge it, rub it out.

Slouching on a groyne
we are big as the storms that split it
tore away promenade, concert hall.

The council want it downed.
It is filthy with cooled fires
too many swimmers reaching its stilts
imprinting their hands with its crust
bumping fingers over limpets, barnacled rust.

We want to admire it in watercolour
and pick its last legs from the seabed.

At Cannop Ponds

we take the wettest path.
A nestbox spits a nuthatch.

Dad says they shape the hole
by nibbling it larger then rimming the edge
with mud to keep woodpeckers out.

I ask about sinews in the black beech.
He tells me most trees have a twist in them
changing position for light.
We both press palms against the bark.

Mud sucks our boots, moss is juicy
every tread squeezing
a moat around the foot.

On the jetty a fisherman spins a plastic fish
tricking carp, pike, tench,
bream, perch, gudgeon.

We pause over water
clear spaces where silt is settled
crowfoot birthing silver beads.

He can still name every fish, plant
bird, tree, starting with Latin
forgetting I'll insist on the Common.

He shows me a slime mould on an oak stump
props a node on the end of his finger.
Light glows inside.

There is a mackerel head
by the bench where we pause
one platinum eye.

He describes stumps of alder as gorgeous
says their sap must be red
so I look for wounds.

Across the water, coots pop up
an oak shakes off birds and bits of gold.

He says there's more life in the reeds
the yellow smoke of oatgrass.

For him, I want the air peppered with little grebes
lifting and landing on the surface like fleas.

I want to keep asking
make sure he remembers every bird call.

He says he is tired of listing things for me

says, quietly, that he and his mates
used to jump into marl holes.
The Blackhand Gang of 50s Smethwick
finding gaps in the fences
of biscuit factories, building sites
skirting pits of quicklime.

On the biggest rock
we do not find the black crossbow
of the lone Cormorant.

This Pool

I swam here with a woman
who told me secrets.

In a pool the colour of ale
we admired our underwater arms.

Our breath dissolved
with minerals and ferric salts.

She let water slip
over her lower lip
mix with her story
of the woman she left him for.

Swimming sideways
we crossed the middle
colder, darker water
where we could not see the weeds.

I allowed myself a sip
tasted iron.

Water sucked us smooth
her tufty hair a slick, black cap
near the place where
water scrambled with air.

Our lips dipping
breaching surface tension
she told me secrets.

Free Morning

Finally, I had time
to watch pigeons roosting in a line
sleeping, gargling air, breaths sour with fumes
while below them twin doors swung, spat suits
twin-sets.

I saw no-one else lift their head, to notice them
ranged along the flat roof of a narrow, white pub
smooth, mottled, like a row of pebbles.

My skin cooled
against the backrest of a chrome chair
as they unpeeled redcurrent eyes, scanned for hawks
in a sky the blue and white shades
of pack-ice.

A polystyrene cup gave its heat to my hands
as I placed my eyes among them
searched out the emerald in their throats

and while I paused there
pointed shoes tapped pavements
someone crushed a cup.

Bertha

'They called out to him that she was on the roof, where she was standing, waving her arms, above the battlements' (Jane Eyre, Chapter 36)

I saw her on the flat roof
of the Dower House
where the M32 flows into Bristol
past Pur Down.

Repainted yellow,
though people still describe
the grey asylum
that let slip its inmates.

I saw her where wind hurled gulls
picked at her scribble of hair.

Her white dress flickered between its towers.

Her arms and legs were pale
like watercolour.

I asked you to slow the car and look
but you kept driving.
Fields poured into the curve of your throat.

I watched her meet your lip
slide beneath your cheek

looked back
found her whittled to a small flag.

She was still flickering that night
while you snored

and I closed my eyes to watch her.

Let The Breeze In

Let the breeze in, sister
that's what I would have said, had I known.

Unlock the casement, scrape the latch through its rust
break the stubborn scab

let the Brighton air swipe his photographs
drop its freshly-gathered rain on his apple mac.

Let the breeze in, sister
soak his pictures of other women and empty buildings.

Let the breeze in, sister.

Grandad

Woodsmoke
on a September afternoon
where white light stays a while
and window cleaners hold poles
to reach the higher panes
reminds me of that ink sketch of Littlewoods
Lord Street, where you are a cluster of lines

glass squeaking beneath your scrims and skins
head murmuring Joyce, O'Casey
Songs of the Republic
lines from Yeats misting the glass.

Among the gasps of bus brakes
I load your books into the boot of our van
creases in the covers like swollen veins
spend hours reading your marginalia
pencilled off-shoots in your Joyce

thoughts scattered on a launderette ticket
precious.

Mistress

She stitches a gleam on a lip

winds her wrists in silk
feels her pulse push against the yellow
she may use for sun or corn.

A sea squeezes her fingers.

Most nights
she clears the warp
knows she hasn't got it right

snaps the stiches in their eyes
and smiles

a soft mess in her clenched fist.

His Groom

watches them eat
through the meat's greasy steam.
The thane is slitting chicken.

The loose, white pouch of the old man
wakes remembering scents
smoke, mud, leaves

while his groom can't sleep
dips a taper into the fire
carries a yellow petal to his candle.

He admires his shadow on the walls
hopes the black shapes dripping from the hall
are bats wrapped in their wings

wafts a tiny moth, doesn't know
the lady is spiking his posset
mulling milk with sugar and wine.

While she measures her metaphors
he seals an arrow-slit
with his shadow's hand

proud to have touched a king
to carry him on his finger

like wing dust.

The Word

When he picks up the carton,
expecting weight, a slight tug on muscle,

expecting milk, like white silk
coiling in his coffee

and finds a box of air

he squeezes so hard
corners press red ticks in his palm
box popping a milky burp.

All she sees is a fist of card
lay a weak punch on the bedpost.

All she hears is the word
hurled through the open door.

If you held her head to your ear
like a shell,

you might still hear it.

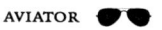

Acknowledgements

'Mistress' was published in *Magma* 59;
'Bertha' was published in the recent *Stony Thursday Book*;
'The Word' was shortlisted for The Bridport Prize;

Thank you to to the editors and judges.

EYEWEAR  AVIATOR

2016 SERIES

CLAIRE WILLIAMSON
Split Ends

ELIZABETH PARKER
Antinopolis

PAUL DEATON
Black Knight

More to come...

WWW.EYEWEARPUBLISHING.COM

Lightning Source UK Ltd.
Milton Keynes UK
UKOW02f1823080316

269849UK00001B/5/P